JADEN CROSS

Cloud Native Development in Go

First edition

This book was professionally typeset on Reedsy.
Find out more at reedsy.com

Contents

Introduction to Cloud-Native Development and Go   1

Building Cloud-Native Applications with Go   4

Containerization and Orchestration with Docker and...   8

Managing State and Data in Cloud-Native Go Applications   12

Implementing Concurrency and Parallelism in Go   17

Security in Cloud-Native Go Applications   23

Observability and Monitoring with Go   28

CI/CD and Deployment Automation   34

Scaling and Optimizing Performance in Production   40

Advanced Topics and Emerging Trends   46

Case Studies and Real-World Applications   52

Troubleshooting and Best Practices   57

Introduction to Cloud-Native Development and Go

1.1 What is Cloud-Native Development?

Begin by defining cloud-native development in clear terms, emphasizing its architecture and methodology designed to leverage cloud platforms. Here, clarify that cloud-native development goes beyond just using the cloud; it's about creating applications optimized for scalability, flexibility, and resilience within a cloud environment. Touch on foundational principles:

- **Microservices Architecture**: Each part of an application operates independently, enhancing modularity and making deployments faster and more manageable.
- **Containerization**: Applications are isolated and packed into containers, promoting consistency across development, testing, and production.
- **Dynamic Orchestration**: Managed by orchestration tools like Kubernetes, cloud-native applications can efficiently scale and adapt to varying workloads.

Discuss the **benefits** of cloud-native development—particularly how it allows teams to innovate, deploy, and scale faster, and increases reliability and resilience against infrastructure failures.

1.2 Why Choose Go for Cloud-Native Development?

Go's strengths align well with cloud-native development's goals of speed, simplicity, and efficiency. Introduce Go's core advantages for cloud-native applications:

- **Concurrency**: Go's goroutines allow highly efficient parallel processing, ideal for distributed systems handling multiple tasks concurrently.
- **Memory Efficiency**: Go's lightweight design is beneficial in cloud environments where resources are shared, and efficient memory usage is essential.
- **Ease of Deployment**: As a statically compiled language, Go produces self-contained binaries, making deployment simpler and reducing dependency issues.
- **Wide Cloud Ecosystem Support**: Describe how Go has become widely used in cloud-native tools, from Kubernetes (written in Go) to Docker, making it a natural fit for developers working in cloud-based environments.

This section should highlight why Go is popular in cloud-native development and how its design philosophy supports building efficient, resilient, and maintainable cloud-native applications.

1.3 Essential Tools and Libraries for Cloud-Native Go

List and describe critical tools and libraries Go developers need for cloud-native development. Introduce Docker and Kubernetes as key tools and explain their relevance to Go developers:

- **Docker**: Describe Docker as an essential containerization tool that allows developers to package Go applications with all necessary dependencies, ensuring consistent deployment across environments.
- **Kubernetes**: Detail Kubernetes as the orchestrator that manages containerized Go applications, covering topics like workload balancing, auto-scaling, and handling failovers.
- **Helm**: Explain Helm's role in managing Kubernetes deployments, providing templated configurations that simplify the process of deploying

and updating applications.
- **Popular Libraries**: Highlight Go-specific libraries that support common cloud-native needs. Examples include:
- Gin or Echo for building RESTful APIs
- gRPC for high-performance, low-latency RPC calls
- Prometheus client for monitoring, providing instrumentation of Go applications.

This section will serve as a resource map, guiding readers on the essential tools they'll use throughout the book.

1.4 Setting Up Your Development Environment

Conclude the chapter by guiding readers through the setup of their Go development environment:

- **Go Installation**: Provide a brief walkthrough for installing Go and setting up their workspace.
- **IDEs and Editors**: Recommend Go-compatible IDEs, such as VS Code and GoLand, explaining how integrated tools like debugging, linting, and auto-completion assist in productivity.
- **Package Management with Go Modules**: Describe Go modules as a system for managing dependencies, which is crucial for creating reproducible builds in cloud-native applications. Explain how modules help manage package versions, ensuring compatibility and stability in a cloud-native context.
- **Docker and Kubernetes CLI**: Guide readers to install Docker and Kubernetes CLI tools, as these will be foundational for development and deployment exercises later in the book.
- **Additional Extensions and Tools**: Mention tools like Delve (for debugging Go applications) and Tilt (for simplifying Kubernetes development workflows), providing readers with the ability to quickly debug, iterate, and deploy their Go applications.

Building Cloud-Native Applications with Go

2.1 Designing Microservices Architecture in Go

Start by introducing the **concept of microservices architecture** and why it's a suitable approach for cloud-native applications. Discuss the advantages of microservices over monolithic structures, such as modularity, scalability, and easier deployment cycles. Outline the specific benefits of designing microservices with Go:

- **Modularity in Go**: Discuss how to structure Go code for modularity, making it easy to separate services by function, e.g., authentication, data processing, etc.
- **Communication Between Services**: Cover options for inter-service communication in a Go microservices environment, including REST APIs and gRPC (addressed in detail later).
- **Fault Isolation and Resilience**: Explain techniques for handling faults within microservices, such as retries, circuit breakers, and fallbacks, enabling resilience and fault isolation.

Describe the best practices for building microservices in Go, including project organization, naming conventions, and the use of Go's lightweight structure to create fast, efficient services.

2.2 Building a RESTful API with Go

In this section, walk readers through developing a robust RESTful API in Go. Begin with an overview of REST principles, including resources, HTTP methods, and status codes. Guide readers through setting up a simple REST API:

- **Setting Up a Simple RESTful API**: Use popular Go frameworks like Gin or Echo to demonstrate how to handle HTTP requests, route management, and JSON responses.
- **Implementing CRUD Operations**: Walk through the steps to create, read, update, and delete resources in the API, covering both the routing setup and basic handlers.
- **Middleware for Security and Logging**: Explain how middleware can improve security and observability by implementing logging, authentication, and error handling in API endpoints.
- **Error Handling and Response Structure**: Provide guidance on structuring API responses, standardizing error messages, and using HTTP status codes effectively for clarity and usability.

Conclude by explaining how RESTful APIs allow microservices to be modular and platform-agnostic, which makes them well-suited to cloud-native applications.

2.3 Working with gRPC for High-Performance Services

Introduce **gRPC** as a high-performance, open-source remote procedure call (RPC) framework particularly suitable for low-latency and high-throughput environments, often essential for cloud-native architectures.

- **Setting Up gRPC in Go**: Explain how to install the necessary packages for gRPC in Go and how to structure a basic gRPC service. Outline steps to create .proto files to define service methods and messages, then show how to compile them for use in Go.
- **Defining and Implementing Service Contracts**: Detail how to define service contracts and message types using Protocol Buffers (.proto files),

with examples of typical request and response messages.

- **Using gRPC vs REST for Cloud-Native Applications**: Compare and contrast REST and gRPC, highlighting where each fits best in a microservices environment. Address performance advantages with gRPC for high-throughput, low-latency use cases, especially for internal microservice communication.
- **Implementing Client-Server Streaming**: Cover advanced gRPC features like client and server streaming, which enable more efficient data transfer for use cases requiring real-time updates or continuous data flows.

Conclude this section with practical examples and guidance on when to choose gRPC over REST in cloud-native applications.

2.4 Hands-On Project: Building a Microservice with REST and gRPC

End this chapter with a hands-on project to bring together the topics covered so far. Guide readers through the process of designing, implementing, and deploying a simple microservice using both RESTful and gRPC interfaces.

- **Project Setup**: Outline the requirements for the project, including Go, Docker, and other dependencies.
- **Designing the Microservice**: Define the functionality of the microservice (e.g., a simple user management system with CRUD operations).
- **Implementing REST Endpoints**: Show how to implement REST endpoints for the service, handling JSON data, routing, and response formatting.
- **Adding gRPC Support**: Convert or add to the service with gRPC methods for the same operations, covering request and response handling in Go.
- **Testing and Deploying**: Provide steps for testing both the RESTful and gRPC endpoints, running the service in Docker, and deploying it locally or to a Kubernetes cluster.
- **Performance Comparison**: Perform basic performance tests on both

the RESTful and gRPC endpoints to showcase the practical differences in throughput and latency.

Containerization and Orchestration with Docker and Kubernetes

3.1 Docker Fundamentals for Go Applications

Introduce Docker as the core tool for containerization, explaining why it's invaluable in cloud-native development. Cover the following key topics:

- **What is Docker and Why Use It?**
- Explain Docker as a platform for packaging applications and their dependencies into containers, which ensures consistency across various environments.
- Discuss the benefits of using Docker for Go applications, particularly the ease of deployment, environment consistency, and streamlined CI/CD processes.
- **Creating and Optimizing Dockerfiles**
- Describe the purpose of a Dockerfile in defining a container's configuration, with specific instructions for Go applications.
- Walk through the creation of a basic Dockerfile for a Go application, focusing on multi-stage builds to keep image sizes small and efficient. Highlight each step:
- **Stage 1 - Build Stage**: Compile the Go application.
- **Stage 2 - Runtime Stage**: Use a lightweight image (e.g., scratch or alpine) to run the binary, reducing the image size significantly.
- Provide tips on avoiding common Dockerfile pitfalls, such as managing unnecessary layers, caching issues, and dependency management.

- **Running and Testing Containers Locally**
- Demonstrate how to build, run, and test Docker containers locally with basic Docker commands. Explain commands like docker build, docker run, and docker exec.
- Offer debugging tips for common issues encountered during container runtime, such as file permissions, environment variable configuration, and networking setup.

3.2 Kubernetes Basics and Deployment

Transition from containerization to orchestration, introducing Kubernetes as the leading tool for managing and scaling containerized applications in a cloud-native environment.

- **Understanding Kubernetes Architecture**
- Provide a high-level overview of Kubernetes components—Pods, Nodes, the Control Plane, and Services—explaining how they work together to manage containers.
- Describe how Kubernetes differs from Docker, positioning Kubernetes as a tool for orchestrating containers at scale, managing clusters, and providing resilience.
- **Deploying Go Applications on Kubernetes**
- Walk through deploying a simple Go application on Kubernetes, starting with defining Kubernetes manifests for deployment.
- **Creating a Pod**: Show how to create a basic Pod definition and then expand to use Deployments for managing multiple replicas.
- **Service Definitions**: Explain Kubernetes Services, which enable external access to applications running within the cluster. Walk through setting up a Service for the Go application.
- **Managing Configurations with ConfigMaps and Secrets**
- Explain how to use ConfigMaps for non-sensitive configuration data, such as environment variables, and Secrets for sensitive information like database passwords or API keys.
- Provide practical examples of using ConfigMaps and Secrets with Go

applications, demonstrating how they can help manage configurations dynamically.

3.3 Kubernetes Advanced: Scaling, Rollouts, and Autoscaling

Dive deeper into advanced Kubernetes concepts that are essential for managing applications in production.

- **Horizontal Scaling with Replicas**
- Explain the concept of scaling in Kubernetes and how to adjust replicas to handle increased load.
- Walk through a scaling example, showing how to increase or decrease the number of replicas for a Go service based on traffic demands.
- **Managing Rolling Updates and Rollbacks**
- Describe Kubernetes' rolling update strategy, which allows for zero-downtime deployments by gradually updating Pods.
- Show how to configure and trigger a rolling update for a Go application, and explain how Kubernetes manages rollbacks in case of deployment issues.
- **Autoscaling with the Horizontal Pod Autoscaler**
- Introduce the Horizontal Pod Autoscaler (HPA), which automatically adjusts the number of replicas based on CPU utilization or other metrics.
- Walk through setting up HPA for a Go application and discuss best practices for configuring autoscaling thresholds, explaining how autoscaling helps maintain application performance while optimizing resource usage.

3.4 Hands-On Project: Containerizing and Orchestrating a Go Microservice

To reinforce the concepts covered, conclude this chapter with a hands-on project that combines Docker and Kubernetes skills.

- **Project Overview and Setup**: Define the microservice to be containerized and orchestrated—such as a simple REST API that responds with data.

- **Step-by-Step Dockerization**:
- Create a Dockerfile for the Go microservice, focusing on a multi-stage build.
- Test the Docker image locally, covering any common troubleshooting steps.
- **Kubernetes Deployment Setup**:
- Define Kubernetes manifests for the microservice deployment and service configuration, ensuring readers understand each component (Pods, Deployments, Services).
- Walk through deploying the microservice on a local Kubernetes cluster using Minikube or Docker Desktop's Kubernetes feature.
- **Scaling and Monitoring**:
- Enable Horizontal Pod Autoscaler for the deployment, configure scaling thresholds, and monitor the service's response to simulated traffic spikes.
- Show how to monitor the deployment's performance using basic Kubernetes tools (kubectl top command or Kubernetes Dashboard).
- **Troubleshooting and Debugging**:
- Include common troubleshooting tips for deployment errors, issues with autoscaling, and Dockerfile misconfigurations.
- Suggest tools and commands for debugging container and network issues within Kubernetes, such as kubectl logs, kubectl describe, and kubectl exec.

Managing State and Data in Cloud-Native Go Applications

4.1 Databases and Data Storage in Cloud-Native Go

Start with an overview of data storage options for cloud-native applications, highlighting the distinction between **SQL** and **NoSQL databases**. Discuss when each is suitable for different types of cloud-native applications, as well as Go's compatibility with various databases:

- **Integrating SQL Databases (e.g., PostgreSQL, MySQL)**
- Introduce popular SQL databases like PostgreSQL and MySQL and their common uses in microservices and transactional applications.
- Walk through setting up a database connection in Go using a popular library like pgx for PostgreSQL or gorm for ORM-based interactions.
- Cover the basics of creating, reading, updating, and deleting (CRUD) operations in Go, and discuss best practices for efficiently interacting with SQL databases in a cloud environment.
- **Working with NoSQL Databases (e.g., MongoDB, Redis)**
- Explain the benefits of NoSQL databases like MongoDB for document storage and Redis for in-memory data caching, ideal for scenarios requiring fast, scalable, and flexible data models.
- Demonstrate setting up and connecting a Go application to MongoDB and Redis, discussing typical use cases for each.
- Guide readers through basic CRUD operations with MongoDB and explore caching data with Redis to reduce database load and latency.

12

- **Data Consistency, Availability, and Partitioning**
- Discuss CAP theorem (Consistency, Availability, and Partition Tolerance) as it relates to cloud-native applications, helping readers understand trade-offs between data consistency and availability.
- Offer practical advice on managing consistency and availability requirements when using distributed databases in cloud-native environments, especially for high-availability applications.

4.2 Caching Strategies for Improved Performance

Introduce the role of caching in cloud-native applications, especially in Go-based microservices that require optimized performance:

- **Why Caching Matters in Cloud-Native Go Applications**
- Describe the benefits of caching, particularly for reducing load on primary databases and improving application response times.
- Explain caching in the context of cloud-native applications, emphasizing how a well-implemented caching strategy can contribute to the scalability and efficiency of microservices.
- **In-Memory Caching with Redis**
- Walk through setting up and configuring Redis as an in-memory cache for Go applications, discussing common use cases (e.g., session management, API caching).
- Cover strategies for caching different types of data (e.g., user sessions, frequently accessed data) and demonstrate how to implement basic caching operations in Go with the Redis client library.
- Provide examples of TTL (time-to-live) settings and eviction policies to ensure efficient cache usage and prevent stale data from persisting too long.
- **Distributed Caching Techniques**
- Introduce distributed caching techniques for horizontally scaling caches across multiple nodes, which is especially relevant for large-scale applications.
- Discuss tools and approaches for setting up distributed caching with

Redis or Memcached in a Kubernetes environment, which can help prevent cache bottlenecks and ensure that cached data remains accessible under heavy loads.
- Provide a code example for using consistent hashing or sharding, ensuring that cache data is balanced across instances.

4.3 Managing State in Stateless Architectures

Dive into the challenges and solutions for handling state in cloud-native environments where stateless services are preferred.

- **Understanding Stateless vs. Stateful Services**
- Explain the benefits of stateless services in cloud-native applications, including scalability and simplified resource management.
- Discuss the limitations of stateless architectures, particularly for applications that need to maintain user sessions or transactional data across multiple services.
- **Techniques for Managing Sessions in Stateless Services**
- Discuss strategies for session management without relying on server memory, including using cookies, tokens (JWTs), and external storage solutions.
- Walk through implementing session management using JWTs in Go, covering how to store session information securely on the client side while minimizing state requirements on the server.
- Provide examples of external session storage solutions, such as Redis or a dedicated session management service, to help persist user session data across multiple instances.
- **Handling Persistent Data in Microservices**
- Introduce patterns for managing persistent data in stateless environments, such as the **Database-per-Service** and **Event Sourcing** patterns.
- Describe how to structure data in microservices to allow each service to manage its own data independently, which aids in avoiding direct dependencies between services.
- Discuss how event sourcing allows for tracking state changes by record-

14

ing events, providing a reliable audit trail and enabling rollback capabilities.

4.4 Data Replication and Backup in Cloud-Native Environments

Discuss best practices for replicating and backing up data, especially in distributed, cloud-native environments.

- **Data Replication for High Availability**
- Describe data replication strategies to ensure data availability, even during failures or outages. Cover **master-slave** and **multi-master** replication and when to use each.
- Explain how to set up data replication for SQL databases like PostgreSQL and NoSQL databases like MongoDB, with considerations for balancing consistency and availability.
- **Automating Backups in Cloud-Native Applications**
- Outline the importance of automated backups for disaster recovery, especially for persistent data in cloud-native applications.
- Discuss backup options for cloud-native environments, such as snapshots and scheduled backups for SQL and NoSQL databases.
- Provide an example of automating backups with a cloud provider's native services (e.g., AWS RDS backups) and open-source tools, demonstrating how Go can trigger these backups via APIs.
- **Handling Data Failover and Recovery**
- Explain data failover mechanisms, ensuring that applications can switch to a replica or secondary database in case of failure.
- Offer guidance on implementing failover in a Kubernetes environment, showing how tools like Kubernetes StatefulSets and cloud-native database replication services can simplify the failover process.
- Conclude this section with an example of creating a failover mechanism for a Go application, illustrating steps for minimizing downtime.

4.5 Hands-On Project: Implementing a Scalable Data Layer in Go

This hands-on project will bring together the chapter's concepts by implementing a data layer that integrates a primary database, caching layer, and state management solutions for a microservice.

- **Project Overview and Setup**: Define a scalable data layer for a sample microservice (e.g., a user profile service), which includes database storage, caching, and session management.
- **Setting Up a Database Layer**:
- Demonstrate the setup of a SQL database (e.g., PostgreSQL) with a Go application and implement basic CRUD operations for storing and retrieving user data.
- Show how to handle database connections and configure connection pooling to support high concurrency.
- **Adding Redis Caching**:
- Implement Redis caching for frequently accessed user profile data, illustrating how to cache and retrieve data efficiently.
- Guide readers through cache expiration and eviction strategies to maintain a balance between cache performance and data freshness.
- **Implementing Stateless Session Management**:
- Implement JWT-based session management, showing how to handle user authentication without storing session state on the server.
- Provide code samples for issuing and verifying tokens, demonstrating how to persist session data without compromising the stateless architecture.
- **Testing Data Replication and Failover**:
- Guide readers in configuring basic data replication for the database, simulating a failover scenario to ensure continuity.
- Show how to test failover readiness by triggering a manual failover and observing the microservice's response, ensuring the system continues to function with minimal interruption.

Implementing Concurrency and Parallelism in Go

5.1 Understanding Concurrency in Go

Begin by defining concurrency and parallelism, clarifying the distinction and why both are important for cloud-native applications:

- **Concurrency vs. Parallelism**: Explain that **concurrency** refers to structuring code so that multiple tasks can progress, while **parallelism** refers to executing multiple tasks simultaneously. Highlight how Go's approach to concurrency optimizes performance in applications that need to handle multiple requests or operations at once.
- **Why Go Excels at Concurrency**: Describe Go's unique approach to concurrency with goroutines and channels, which makes it lightweight and more manageable than traditional threads. Discuss how Go's concurrency model is suited to cloud-native applications, where scaling efficiently is a priority.
- **Concurrency and the Go Scheduler**: Provide a brief overview of the Go scheduler, which handles the distribution of goroutines across available CPU cores. Explain how this differs from traditional OS thread scheduling and why it makes Go highly efficient for concurrent applications.

5.2 Goroutines and Channels in Go

This section introduces the foundational building blocks for concurrency in Go: **goroutines** and **channels**.

- **Using Goroutines to Run Concurrent Tasks**
- Explain what a goroutine is and how it functions as a lightweight thread managed by the Go runtime.
- Provide a basic example of launching a goroutine and describe the go keyword, demonstrating how easy it is to implement concurrent functions.
- Discuss the concept of goroutine stack sizes and how Go dynamically adjusts memory allocation, making goroutines resource-efficient.
- **Communicating Between Goroutines with Channels**
- Describe channels as Go's mechanism for safely sharing data between goroutines without requiring traditional locks.
- Walk through creating and using channels, covering both **unbuffered** and **buffered channels**. Include examples showing how data flows between goroutines using channels.
- Discuss common patterns such as **fan-in** (multiple goroutines sending to one channel) and **fan-out** (one goroutine sending to multiple goroutines), which are essential for parallel processing of tasks.
- **Synchronization with Select Statements**
- Introduce the select statement as a way to wait for multiple channel operations, allowing more complex synchronization between goroutines.
- Provide examples of using select to implement timeouts, prioritize tasks, and coordinate the flow of data across channels.

5.3 Patterns for Concurrent Cloud-Native Applications

Explore specific patterns and techniques for structuring concurrent tasks in Go, particularly within cloud-native applications.

- **Worker Pools for Task Management**
- Explain the **worker pool** pattern, where a fixed number of worker goroutines handle tasks from a shared job queue. This approach is effective for rate-limiting or load-balancing tasks.

- Walk through implementing a worker pool in Go, using channels to dispatch tasks and gather results.
- Discuss use cases for worker pools in cloud-native environments, such as managing background tasks, handling HTTP requests, or processing data streams.
- **Pipelines for Streamlined Data Processing**
- Describe the **pipeline** pattern, where tasks are broken down into stages, with each stage represented by a goroutine. Data flows between stages through channels.
- Provide an example of a pipeline for processing data, such as transforming and filtering a stream of data.
- Discuss benefits like modularity and separation of concerns, which are useful for building scalable and maintainable cloud-native applications.
- **Fan-In/Fan-Out Patterns for High-Throughput Systems**
- Explain **fan-in** and **fan-out** patterns, which allow distributing tasks across multiple goroutines (fan-out) and aggregating results (fan-in).
- Demonstrate these patterns in the context of cloud-native applications, such as processing high volumes of data or handling multiple incoming requests.
- Provide best practices for using these patterns effectively, including avoiding deadlocks, ensuring graceful shutdowns, and monitoring resource usage.

5.4 Common Concurrency Pitfalls and Solutions

Highlight some typical pitfalls developers face with concurrency in Go and provide solutions.

- **Race Conditions and Data Races**
- Explain race conditions and how they occur when two or more goroutines access shared data concurrently without synchronization.
- Demonstrate how to use Go's **race detector** to identify data races and explain solutions, such as using channels or the sync.Mutex package for locking shared resources.

- Provide best practices for avoiding race conditions, emphasizing the advantages of using channels over locks for synchronization.
- **Deadlocks and How to Avoid Them**
- Define deadlocks, which occur when goroutines are stuck waiting indefinitely for resources.
- Explain how deadlocks happen, particularly with improper use of channels or circular dependencies between goroutines.
- Offer techniques to prevent deadlocks, such as careful design of channel communication, using buffered channels, and applying timeouts to channel operations with select.
- **Managing Resource Usage with Goroutines**
- Discuss potential issues with launching too many goroutines, which can lead to high memory and CPU usage.
- Provide strategies for limiting the number of goroutines, such as using worker pools and controlling goroutine lifecycles.
- Include a section on monitoring goroutines, explaining how to inspect goroutine counts with debugging tools and optimize resource usage.

5.5 High-Performance Go for Cloud Workloads

In this section, focus on optimizing concurrency for high-performance applications, which is essential for cloud-native development.

- **Optimizing CPU and Memory Usage**
- Discuss strategies for reducing CPU and memory usage in concurrent Go applications, particularly in resource-limited cloud environments.
- Describe how to monitor and optimize goroutine usage, including techniques for profiling CPU and memory usage in Go applications.
- **Using Context for Cancellation and Timeout Control**
- Introduce Go's context package, which is invaluable for managing timeouts and cancellations in concurrent operations.
- Demonstrate how to use context.Context to propagate deadlines, time-outs, and cancellation signals across goroutines, particularly in web server applications or long-running processes.

- Provide a code example showing how to set up and use contexts, ensuring that resources are released when goroutines finish.
- **Profiling and Benchmarking Concurrency**
- Cover Go's profiling tools, such as pprof, which allow developers to benchmark and optimize concurrent code.
- Walk through a basic example of profiling a concurrent application, identifying performance bottlenecks, and interpreting profiling data to make improvements.
- Discuss common optimization strategies, such as reducing contention on shared resources and fine-tuning goroutine creation and destruction.

5.6 Hands-On Project: Building a Concurrent Task Processor in Go

This hands-on project will combine all the concurrency concepts covered, guiding readers through building a concurrent task processor for a sample cloud-native application.

- **Project Overview and Setup**: Define a concurrent task processor that handles a large number of tasks, such as processing requests or performing data transformations.
- **Implementing Worker Pools**:
- Set up a worker pool with a configurable number of workers to manage the task load.
- Use channels to manage the queue of incoming tasks, demonstrating how to distribute tasks efficiently across workers.
- **Adding a Fan-Out/Fan-In Pipeline**:
- Integrate a fan-out/fan-in structure to handle tasks that require multiple stages of processing.
- Demonstrate how to split a task into subtasks, distribute them across workers, and then gather the results for further processing.
- **Implementing Cancellation and Timeouts with Contexts**:
- Add timeout controls to the task processor, using context.Context to manage long-running or stalled tasks.
- Show how to handle cancellations gracefully, ensuring that resources are

released and tasks are stopped when necessary.

- **Testing and Benchmarking**:
- Guide readers through testing and benchmarking the task processor to measure performance and identify bottlenecks.
- Use pprof to profile the application and demonstrate optimizations based on profiling data.

Security in Cloud-Native Go Applications

6.1 Secure API Development with Go

Start by discussing the critical importance of securing APIs in cloud-native applications. Cover essential API security concepts and techniques for Go applications:

- **Authentication and Authorization**
- Define authentication (verifying user identity) and authorization (defining user permissions), explaining their significance in protecting resources.
- Introduce **JWT (JSON Web Tokens)** as a popular approach for stateless authentication. Walk readers through generating, validating, and parsing JWTs in Go to authorize API requests.
- Explain **OAuth 2.0** and its use cases, especially for integrating third-party services. Provide an example of setting up OAuth 2.0 with a Go application, emphasizing access tokens and refresh tokens.
- **Implementing Role-Based Access Control (RBAC)**
- Describe role-based access control as a method for restricting access based on user roles. Provide examples of how to define user roles (e.g., admin, user, guest) and enforce permissions at the API level.
- Walk readers through a basic RBAC implementation in Go, demonstrating how to manage roles and permissions in middleware.
- **Rate Limiting and Throttling**
- Explain the importance of rate limiting in preventing abuse, DoS attacks, and resource exhaustion.

- Demonstrate how to implement rate limiting in Go using middleware and libraries, covering strategies like **fixed window** and **sliding window** algorithms.
- Discuss how to integrate with external rate-limiting services or APIs, especially in distributed applications.

6.2 Data Encryption and Secure Storage

Discuss the necessity of data encryption to protect sensitive information in cloud-native applications. Focus on encryption practices suitable for both data in transit and data at rest:

- **Encrypting Data in Transit**
- Explain the importance of securing data as it travels between services, especially in distributed environments.
- Discuss the role of **TLS (Transport Layer Security)** in protecting data in transit and walk readers through enabling TLS in Go APIs. Provide examples of setting up HTTPS in Go applications using certificates.
- Cover mutual TLS (mTLS) for cases where both client and server need authentication, such as secure inter-service communication.
- **Encrypting Data at Rest**
- Describe methods for encrypting data at rest, including file encryption and database encryption.
- Show how to use Go's crypto package to encrypt sensitive data before storage, such as user information or secrets.
- Discuss best practices for managing encryption keys, including using cloud-managed key services (e.g., AWS KMS, Google Cloud KMS) for automatic key rotation and secure storage.
- **Hashing Passwords Securely**
- Emphasize the importance of password hashing over encryption for storing user passwords.
- Walk through implementing secure password hashing in Go using libraries like bcrypt, including examples of hashing and verifying passwords.

- Discuss considerations like choosing the right hashing algorithm and adjusting hashing strength to balance security and performance.

6.3 Hardening Container Security

Since containerization is fundamental to cloud-native applications, this section covers security measures for containers running Go applications:

- **Securing Docker Images**
- Explain the importance of creating secure Docker images, including reducing image size and removing unnecessary dependencies.
- Introduce **multi-stage builds** as a method for keeping Docker images lean and minimizing the attack surface. Provide examples of best practices for writing secure Dockerfiles, such as using official base images and specifying non-root users.
- Show how to scan Docker images for vulnerabilities using tools like **Trivy** or **Clair**, which identify outdated dependencies and security risks.
- **Applying Runtime Security in Kubernetes**
- Discuss container runtime security settings in Kubernetes, such as **Pod Security Policies** (PSPs) and the newer **Pod Security Standards**.
- Walk through setting resource limits, restricting privileged access, and defining security contexts in Kubernetes manifests.
- Introduce **Open Policy Agent (OPA)** or **Kyverno** as tools for enforcing policies and ensuring security compliance across Kubernetes clusters.
- **Managing Secrets Securely**
- Explain the risks of embedding sensitive information (e.g., passwords, API keys) in code or configuration files.
- Demonstrate how to securely manage secrets in Kubernetes using **Kubernetes Secrets,** which securely stores sensitive data and controls access.
- Cover integration with external secrets management tools (e.g., HashiCorp Vault, AWS Secrets Manager), showing how Go applications can retrieve secrets at runtime.

6.4 Monitoring and Logging for Security

Highlight the importance of monitoring and logging as part of a security strategy, enabling visibility into application behavior and potential security incidents.

- **Logging Best Practices for Security**
- Discuss best practices for logging, such as avoiding sensitive information in logs and using structured logging for clarity.
- Show how to implement structured logging in Go using libraries like Logrus or Zap, including examples of logging request metadata (IP address, user agent) for security auditing.
- Cover compliance considerations, such as anonymizing or encrypting personally identifiable information (PII) in logs.
- **Monitoring for Intrusion Detection**
- Explain the need for intrusion detection in cloud-native applications to identify suspicious activities and prevent breaches.
- Introduce common tools for monitoring security events in Go applications, such as **Prometheus** and **Grafana** for alerting on unusual patterns, or **Falco** for runtime security monitoring in Kubernetes.
- Describe how to set up alerts based on specific security events, like failed login attempts or rate limit triggers.
- **Distributed Tracing for Security Analysis**
- Explain how distributed tracing aids in tracking requests across microservices, providing visibility into potential vulnerabilities in the system.
- Walk through setting up tracing in Go with **OpenTelemetry** to monitor the flow of data across services and identify potential security weaknesses.
- Discuss how distributed tracing helps in investigating breaches or unusual behavior, particularly in complex cloud-native architectures.

6.5 Hands-On Project: Securing a Go API for Cloud-Native Deployment

To put these security concepts into practice, guide readers through building a secure Go API with security features tailored for a cloud-native environment.

- **Project Overview and Setup**: Define a REST API for a sample cloud-native service (e.g., an e-commerce backend) and outline the security requirements.
- **Implementing Authentication and Role-Based Access Control**:
- Add JWT-based authentication and role-based authorization to secure endpoints. Define roles and enforce permissions on sensitive routes.
- Demonstrate API access control using middleware, showing how to verify JWT tokens and restrict access by user role.
- **Securing Data with Encryption and Hashing**:
- Implement encryption for sensitive fields, such as user credit card information, using Go's crypto package.
- Hash passwords securely with bcrypt, demonstrating password storage best practices.
- **Container Hardening and Deployment in Kubernetes**:
- Create a secure Dockerfile with a multi-stage build to containerize the API.
- Define Kubernetes manifests with security contexts, configuring resource limits, non-root users, and restricted privileges.
- Set up Kubernetes Secrets for managing API keys and database credentials, explaining how to inject them into the container environment securely.
- **Logging and Monitoring**:
- Implement structured logging and configure logging levels to capture security-relevant events.
- Integrate Prometheus and Grafana for monitoring, setting up alerts for potential security issues, such as failed login attempts or unusual traffic spikes.
- Demonstrate how to use distributed tracing to monitor request flows and detect anomalies.

Observability and Monitoring with Go

7.1 Introduction to Observability in Cloud Environments

Start with an overview of observability, explaining its significance in cloud-native applications where services are distributed, and understanding system behavior is essential:

- **Defining Observability**: Explain observability as the capability to measure the internal states of a system based on its outputs (logs, metrics, and traces). Emphasize the difference between observability and monitoring—observability encompasses monitoring but provides a more comprehensive view of system behavior.
- **Why Observability Matters for Cloud-Native Applications**: Discuss how distributed microservices architectures complicate understanding system health. Emphasize the need for observability to pinpoint issues across services, assess latency, and manage system resilience in complex cloud-native environments.
- **The Three Pillars of Observability**:
- **Metrics**: Quantitative measures like response time, error rate, and CPU usage.
- **Logs**: Records of discrete events that capture state changes, errors, and application flows.
- **Traces**: End-to-end tracking of requests across microservices, providing insight into request flow and latency.

7.2 Logging, Monitoring, and Tracing in Go

This section provides a deep dive into implementing the three pillars of observability within Go applications.

- **Implementing Structured Logging in Go**
- Describe the importance of structured logging in cloud-native applications for improved searchability, filtering, and analysis.
- Demonstrate logging in Go with libraries like Logrus or Zap, showing how to include metadata (e.g., request IDs, user IDs) for context.
- Cover best practices for log levels (DEBUG, INFO, WARN, ERROR) and explain how they help separate routine logs from error logs.
- **Metrics Collection with Prometheus**
- Introduce **Prometheus** as a leading tool for metrics collection and monitoring in cloud-native environments.
- Walk through setting up Prometheus for a Go application using the prometheus/client_golang library, covering essential metrics like request counts, latency, and error rates.
- Provide examples of custom application metrics, such as the number of active users, API response times, or cache hit rates, to demonstrate how custom metrics offer deeper insights.
- Cover how to expose metrics through an HTTP endpoint for Prometheus scraping, discussing best practices for metrics naming conventions and labels.
- **Distributed Tracing with OpenTelemetry**
- Explain distributed tracing and its importance in tracking requests across services, which is especially valuable for debugging performance issues and identifying latency bottlenecks.
- Introduce **OpenTelemetry** as a unified framework for distributed tracing, highlighting its support for tracing, metrics, and logging.
- Demonstrate how to instrument a Go application with OpenTelemetry, covering steps to set up a tracer, define spans, and trace a request through multiple microservices.
- Discuss how to connect OpenTelemetry with tracing backends like **Jaeger** or **Zipkin** to visualize request flows and identify slow services.

7.3 Setting Up Monitoring Dashboards

Once metrics and traces are collected, setting up monitoring dashboards enables ongoing visibility into the application's health and performance.

- **Creating a Prometheus Dashboard with Grafana**
- Introduce **Grafana** as a visualization tool compatible with Prometheus metrics, used to create dashboards that monitor system metrics.
- Guide readers through setting up a basic Grafana dashboard for a Go application, connecting Prometheus as the data source.
- Demonstrate creating custom panels to monitor critical metrics, such as error rates, latency distributions, and resource usage (CPU and memory).
- Discuss best practices for dashboard design, such as grouping metrics by service, avoiding clutter, and using alerts to highlight critical issues.
- **Alerting with Prometheus and Grafana**
- Cover the basics of setting up alerts in Prometheus based on predefined conditions, such as high error rates or response time thresholds.
- Walk through configuring alerts to send notifications via email, Slack, or other channels using **Alertmanager**.
- Provide practical advice on setting thresholds and reducing alert noise to avoid alert fatigue, focusing on setting actionable, high-priority alerts for significant issues.

7.4 Distributed Tracing for Microservices Debugging

This section covers advanced distributed tracing techniques tailored for debugging and improving microservices performance.

- **Tracing Across Multiple Services**
- Explain how to propagate trace context across microservices, allowing a single request to be traced from the entry point to the final response.
- Show how to implement context propagation in Go using OpenTelemetry, demonstrating how spans connect to form a complete trace for requests moving through several microservices.
- Provide examples of typical issues identified through tracing, such as

services with high latency or unexpected bottlenecks.
- **Analyzing Latency and Dependency Graphs**
- Discuss how to use traces to analyze latency at each service, identifying where most time is spent.
- Explain how distributed tracing tools like Jaeger or Zipkin provide dependency graphs that show the flow of requests through services, making it easier to identify potential dependencies that impact performance.
- Cover strategies for visualizing latency distributions and service dependencies to help prioritize optimizations effectively.
- **Improving Performance Based on Trace Data**
- Provide actionable steps to improve performance based on trace analysis, such as optimizing SQL queries, reducing inter-service communication, or implementing caching.
- Discuss how to use trace sampling to reduce the amount of tracing data collected while retaining enough detail to identify and diagnose issues in production environments.

7.5 Observability Best Practices for Go Applications

Offer readers best practices for managing observability in Go applications, focusing on practical guidance for achieving long-term reliability and maintaining system health.

- **Setting Up Log Aggregation**
- Describe the importance of centralizing logs in cloud-native applications, particularly when working with multiple services across distributed environments.
- Walk through setting up log aggregation using tools like **ELK Stack (Elasticsearch, Logstash, Kibana)** or **Loki**. Discuss the benefits of centralized log storage for search, filtering, and retention.
- **Managing Metrics and Traces in Production**
- Discuss the importance of fine-tuning the level of detail in logs, metrics, and traces for production environments to avoid performance degradation and storage issues.

- Cover techniques for optimizing Prometheus queries and reducing the cardinality of metrics to improve system performance.
- Explain trace sampling and downsampling techniques to ensure that traces remain manageable without sacrificing valuable insight.
- **Incident Management and Observability**
- Describe how observability integrates with incident management, enabling teams to respond to issues quickly by providing the necessary data for diagnosis.
- Explain how to create runbooks or predefined procedures that leverage observability tools for troubleshooting common issues, such as latency spikes or error rate increases.

7.6 Hands-On Project: Implementing an Observability Suite for a Go Microservice

This hands-on project will provide readers with practical experience setting up a complete observability suite for a Go microservice, covering logging, metrics, and tracing.

- **Project Overview and Setup**: Define a microservice with multiple endpoints to monitor. The project setup should include dependencies on Prometheus, Grafana, and OpenTelemetry for a complete observability stack.
- **Structured Logging Implementation**:
- Set up structured logging in the microservice using Logrus or Zap, including metadata like request IDs, timestamps, and user IDs.
- Demonstrate different log levels and discuss how to log meaningful information that assists in troubleshooting.
- **Setting Up Prometheus Metrics**:
- Implement custom metrics in the Go application, such as request latency and error rates, using Prometheus client libraries.
- Expose these metrics through an HTTP endpoint and configure Prometheus to scrape the data for visualization.
- **Adding Distributed Tracing with OpenTelemetry**:

- Integrate OpenTelemetry to enable distributed tracing across service endpoints, setting up spans to monitor request flows.
- Walk through configuring the tracing backend with Jaeger, visualizing request paths and pinpointing latency bottlenecks.
- **Creating a Monitoring Dashboard in Grafana**:
- Connect Prometheus to Grafana and create a monitoring dashboard that visualizes the microservice's metrics.
- Add panels to track essential metrics (e.g., error rate, latency), setting up alerts in Grafana for key metrics to notify the team of any issues.

CI/CD and Deployment Automation

8.1 CI/CD Pipelines for Go Applications

Begin by defining CI/CD and explaining its importance in the development lifecycle of cloud-native applications:

- **What is CI/CD?**
- Define Continuous Integration (CI) as the practice of frequently merging code changes and running automated tests, ensuring early detection of issues.
- Define Continuous Delivery (CD) as the automated process of preparing software for release, and Continuous Deployment as the further step of automatically deploying every change that passes testing.
- Discuss the benefits of CI/CD for cloud-native applications, including faster feedback loops, improved quality control, and seamless deployment in production.
- **Setting Up CI Pipelines for Go with GitHub Actions**
- Introduce **GitHub Actions** as a flexible and popular CI/CD tool for automating workflows.
- Walk through configuring a basic CI pipeline for a Go application that includes steps like code linting, running tests, and building a Go binary. Cover the setup for each action:
- **Code Linting**: Show how to automate static code analysis using tools like golint or golangci-lint.
- **Running Tests**: Demonstrate how to run Go's built-in testing suite as part of the pipeline, ensuring code quality and functionality.

- **Building Artifacts**: Guide readers in configuring actions to build Go binaries as release artifacts, making them available for deployment.
- Discuss best practices for structuring CI workflows, such as keeping workflows modular and using environment-specific configurations.
- **Implementing Continuous Delivery with GitLab CI**
- Introduce **GitLab CI** as another powerful tool for CI/CD pipelines, with particular advantages for integrating with GitLab repositories.
- Walk through creating a .gitlab-ci.yml configuration file to automate the build, test, and delivery steps.
- Provide examples for setting up pipeline stages, using artifacts for build outputs, and adding deployment steps.
- Explain how GitLab CI integrates with cloud services like Kubernetes, making it easy to deploy applications in a cloud-native environment.

8.2 Infrastructure as Code (IaC) for Cloud Deployments

Introduce the concept of Infrastructure as Code, an essential practice for automating infrastructure setup in cloud-native environments.

- **Why Use Infrastructure as Code?**
- Explain how IaC allows developers to define infrastructure configurations in code, enabling consistency, repeatability, and version control. Discuss how IaC aligns well with CI/CD by making infrastructure setup part of automated workflows.
- Describe the benefits of IaC for cloud-native applications, especially in multi-environment setups (development, testing, production) where consistency is crucial.
- **Using Terraform for Infrastructure Provisioning**
- Introduce **Terraform** as a popular IaC tool that allows declarative configuration for managing cloud resources.
- Walk through setting up a simple infrastructure configuration in Terraform, such as creating a Kubernetes cluster on a cloud provider (e.g., AWS EKS or GCP GKE).
- Cover Terraform basics: defining resources, modules, state management,

and how to write reusable code for managing infrastructure.

- Provide an example of automating the creation of a load balancer, networking setup, and storage provisioning for a Go application.
- **Kubernetes Configurations with Helm**
- Explain how **Helm** simplifies Kubernetes deployments by using charts to package and deploy applications as collections of YAML configurations.
- Demonstrate creating a Helm chart for a Go application, organizing deployment files into templates and values for easy customization.
- Cover how to manage different environments with Helm values files and how to version Helm charts for consistent releases.
- Show how Helm charts integrate with CI/CD pipelines, automating the deployment of Go applications into Kubernetes environments.

8.3 Hands-On Project: Deploying a Go Microservice on Kubernetes

To solidify the concepts covered, guide readers through a hands-on project that deploys a Go microservice using CI/CD and IaC tools, showcasing the full deployment automation process.

- **Project Overview and Setup**: Define a microservice with a few endpoints, which will be continuously integrated, tested, and deployed automatically into a Kubernetes cluster.
- **Setting Up CI/CD Pipeline with GitHub Actions**
- Create a GitHub Actions workflow to run linting, testing, and build steps for the Go microservice.
- Configure an action to build a Docker image for the microservice and push it to a container registry (e.g., Docker Hub or GitHub Container Registry).
- Explain how to store secrets (e.g., registry credentials) securely using GitHub Secrets.
- **Infrastructure Provisioning with Terraform**
- Set up Terraform configurations to provision a Kubernetes cluster on a cloud provider (e.g., AWS, GCP, or Azure).
- Include configuration for networking, storage, and autoscaling policies

to prepare the cluster for cloud-native workloads.

- Demonstrate running terraform apply to create resources, emphasizing the benefits of using version-controlled configurations for infrastructure.
- **Deploying the Microservice with Helm**
- Create a Helm chart for the Go microservice, setting up Kubernetes deployments, services, and other resources required for deployment.
- Configure environment-specific values in the Helm chart for different deployment stages (e.g., staging, production).
- Show how to use the Helm CLI or GitHub Actions to deploy the Helm chart to the Kubernetes cluster automatically upon successful CI runs.
- **Configuring Rollbacks and Blue-Green Deployments**
- Explain blue-green deployments as a strategy for zero-downtime deployments, allowing gradual traffic shifts between old and new versions of the application.
- Demonstrate how to set up blue-green deployments with Helm by creating separate environments for the new and old versions.
- Cover rollback procedures, showing how Helm simplifies reverting to previous versions if issues are detected.

8.4 Advanced CI/CD Practices for Cloud-Native Go Applications

Discuss more advanced topics that enable readers to scale and optimize their CI/CD pipelines in production environments.

- **Implementing Canary Deployments**
- Introduce canary deployments as a method to deploy new changes gradually, starting with a small portion of users and incrementally increasing traffic.
- Demonstrate how to set up canary deployments with Kubernetes and Istio, using traffic-splitting rules to direct a percentage of traffic to the canary version.
- Discuss monitoring and feedback mechanisms for canary deployments, which allow teams to quickly identify and fix issues before full rollout.
- **Continuous Deployment with ArgoCD**

- Introduce **ArgoCD** as a Kubernetes-native continuous deployment tool, designed for GitOps workflows.
- Explain how ArgoCD uses Git as the source of truth for deployment configurations, automatically syncing with the Kubernetes cluster when configuration changes are pushed to Git.
- Walk through a setup example for ArgoCD, showing how it continuously deploys updates to the Go microservice based on changes in the Git repository.
- **Testing and Validating Deployments with CI/CD**
- Explain best practices for testing within CI/CD pipelines, including running unit tests, integration tests, and end-to-end tests as part of the CI pipeline.
- Discuss tools like **KubeScore** and **kubeval** for validating Kubernetes manifests, ensuring they follow best practices and are deployable.
- Cover how to automate rollback if a deployment fails health checks or if errors are detected in production, maintaining application reliability.

8.5 Monitoring and Optimizing CI/CD Pipelines

Offer best practices for ensuring CI/CD pipelines are optimized and provide actionable insights into deployment performance.

- **Pipeline Optimization Tips**
- Provide tips on optimizing pipeline speed and efficiency, such as using caching strategies, splitting workflows, and avoiding unnecessary steps.
- Explain how to monitor pipeline performance metrics (e.g., build time, deployment time) to identify bottlenecks and optimize step execution.
- **Automated Rollbacks and Self-Healing Deployments**
- Discuss how automated rollbacks work in Kubernetes with health probes and rollback strategies configured in Helm charts or ArgoCD.
- Introduce self-healing deployment practices using Kubernetes features like liveness probes and horizontal pod autoscalers to manage and recover from failures.
- **Managing Secrets in CI/CD**

- Cover best practices for securely managing secrets in CI/CD workflows, such as using encrypted storage and automated secret rotation.
- Introduce tools like **HashiCorp Vault** and **AWS Secrets Manager** for external secret management, explaining how to integrate these with CI/CD pipelines.

8.6 Hands-On Project: Full Deployment of a Scalable Application

This final hands-on project will walk readers through deploying a fully scalable, resilient Go application using CI/CD automation and Kubernetes.

- **Project Overview and Setup**: Define a scalable Go application that includes multiple microservices with dependencies (e.g., database and cache).
- **CI/CD Pipeline for Multi-Service Deployment**
- Set up a CI/CD pipeline with GitHub Actions or GitLab CI to build, test, and package each service as a Docker image.
- Configure workflows to handle dependencies and manage the order of deployments for the multi-service application.
- **Automating Kubernetes Deployment with Helm and Terraform**
- Use Terraform to provision the Kubernetes infrastructure and Helm to deploy all microservices to the Kubernetes cluster.
- Implement blue-green or canary deployments to enable zero-downtime upgrades across services.
- **Testing, Monitoring, and Rollback Configuration**
- Implement automated tests for each service and integrate them into the CI/CD pipeline.
- Set up monitoring with Prometheus and Grafana to track deployment health and performance metrics.
- Configure automated rollback policies based on health checks and deployment feedback, ensuring minimal service disruption in case of failures.

Scaling and Optimizing Performance in Production

9.1 Load Balancing and Traffic Management

Start by explaining the role of load balancing in scaling cloud-native applications, especially when traffic fluctuates or grows.

- **Why Load Balancing Matters in Production**
- Describe load balancing as a means to distribute traffic across multiple instances, reducing bottlenecks and ensuring consistent response times.
- Discuss its importance in high-availability environments, where load balancers reroute traffic away from unhealthy instances, enhancing resilience.
- **Types of Load Balancing**
- Explain **Round-Robin Load Balancing**, where traffic is evenly distributed across instances. Discuss its simplicity and best-use scenarios.
- Discuss **Least Connections Load Balancing** for applications with varied request durations, which directs new traffic to instances with the fewest active connections.
- Cover **Geographic and IP Hash Load Balancing**, used for region-based traffic management and sticky sessions.
- **Setting Up Load Balancing for Go Applications**
- Walk through configuring a basic load balancer, like NGINX or HAProxy, for a Go application deployed across multiple instances.
- Provide a step-by-step guide to setting up a load balancer in Kubernetes

using Kubernetes Services, which support round-robin distribution and external load balancing integrations.

- Discuss cloud provider load balancers (e.g., AWS Elastic Load Balancer or Google Cloud Load Balancing), which simplify scalability by integrating with auto-scaling policies.

9.2 Resource Optimization for Cloud-Native Go Applications

Introduce strategies to optimize resource usage, ensuring applications perform efficiently while minimizing costs.

- **Optimizing CPU and Memory Usage**
- Explain the importance of tuning CPU and memory settings, especially in resource-constrained cloud environments. Discuss the impact of Go's garbage collector and how to tune it with GOGC (garbage collection ratio).
- Walk through strategies for profiling memory usage in Go, using tools like pprof to identify memory leaks and optimize high-usage areas.
- Discuss Go's concurrency model and provide tips on tuning goroutine usage to avoid excessive CPU utilization, especially in high-throughput scenarios.
- **Setting Resource Limits and Requests in Kubernetes**
- Explain Kubernetes' resource limits and requests, which ensure that applications only consume a specified amount of CPU and memory, protecting against over-utilization.
- Provide a step-by-step guide for setting these configurations in Kubernetes manifests, explaining how they help avoid throttling and ensure stable application performance.
- Discuss the role of Kubernetes' Horizontal Pod Autoscaler (HPA), which adjusts the number of instances based on CPU and memory metrics, scaling applications dynamically.
- **Using Caching to Reduce Load**
- Describe caching as a strategy to reduce repetitive database queries or external API calls, which can significantly improve response times and

reduce server load.

- Demonstrate how to implement caching in Go using Redis, covering scenarios for caching frequently accessed data (e.g., session tokens, user profiles).
- Discuss cache expiration policies and cache invalidation strategies, ensuring data freshness while maintaining performance.

9.3 Resilience and Fault Tolerance in Go

Cover resilience patterns that enhance application reliability, particularly in cloud-native environments where failures can occur across distributed services.

- **Implementing Circuit Breakers with Go**
- Explain the **circuit breaker** pattern, where requests are temporarily halted when a dependency is unresponsive, preventing cascading failures.
- Demonstrate how to implement a circuit breaker in Go using the sony/gobreaker library, covering setup, configuration, and fallback strategies.
- Provide best practices for setting thresholds and monitoring circuit breaker states, ensuring timely recovery without unnecessary disruptions.
- **Retries and Exponential Backoff**
- Introduce the **retry** pattern, explaining how it handles transient failures by retrying failed requests.
- Walk through implementing retry logic with exponential backoff in Go, which limits retries to avoid overwhelming the failing service.
- Discuss situations where retries are beneficial and scenarios where they may worsen issues, emphasizing cautious use in distributed systems.
- **Rate Limiting and Throttling**
- Explain rate limiting as a means to control the rate of requests to services, protecting against abuse and reducing overload on resources.
- Demonstrate rate limiting in Go using middleware libraries like golang.or g/x/time/rate or third-party tools like Redis, which can handle dis-

tributed rate limits.

- Discuss how to apply rate limiting at both API and microservice levels, showing how to configure and enforce limits for different types of requests.

9.4 Performance Tuning Techniques for Go Applications

Provide advanced tips for tuning performance in production, enabling Go applications to meet the demands of high-traffic, data-intensive scenarios.

- **Go Profiler and Performance Analysis with pprof**
- Introduce **pprof**, Go's built-in profiler, as an essential tool for identifying performance bottlenecks.
- Demonstrate how to use pprof to collect CPU, memory, and goroutine profiles, providing practical examples of interpreting profiling data to diagnose inefficiencies.
- Discuss common patterns found in performance analysis (e.g., memory leaks, high CPU usage) and how to address them effectively.
- **Optimizing Database Queries**
- Explain how database query performance impacts overall application speed, especially in data-heavy applications.
- Demonstrate best practices for optimizing SQL queries, using prepared statements, and reducing redundant database calls in Go.
- Provide tips for monitoring database performance, showing how to identify slow queries and improve indexing for high-frequency requests.
- **Reducing Latency with Efficient Networking**
- Cover efficient networking practices in Go, including optimizing HTTP/2 for faster request handling and using connection pools for improved network performance.
- Introduce gRPC as an alternative to REST for high-performance, low-latency applications, showing how it minimizes network latency.
- Provide an example of setting up connection pools with Go's HTTP client, demonstrating how to reuse connections to reduce the overhead of establishing new connections.

9.5 Monitoring and Scaling Strategies in Kubernetes

Discuss monitoring strategies that help track the performance and scalability of Go applications in production.

- **Using Kubernetes Metrics for Scaling Decisions**
- Describe Kubernetes' Horizontal Pod Autoscaler (HPA) in more detail, showing how it uses CPU and custom metrics for scaling decisions.
- Walk through configuring HPA with metrics from Prometheus, enabling more precise scaling based on actual application load.
- Discuss the role of Vertical Pod Autoscaler (VPA) for automatically adjusting resource limits and requests, especially useful for workloads with variable resource needs.
- **Service Mesh Integration for Advanced Load Management**
- Explain the benefits of integrating a service mesh like **Istio** or **Linkerd** for advanced traffic control and observability.
- Show how service meshes handle traffic routing, load balancing, and circuit breaking at the network layer, enabling finer control over microservices communication.
- Provide an example of setting up a simple circuit breaker or retry policy within Istio, highlighting how service mesh configurations simplify managing resilience.
- **Configuring Alerts and Dashboards for Production Monitoring**
- Guide readers in setting up Prometheus and Grafana for production monitoring, covering essential dashboards for CPU, memory, and latency metrics.
- Walk through configuring alerts for critical metrics, such as high error rates, increased latency, or failed readiness probes.
- Discuss best practices for alerting, including actionable thresholds, reducing alert noise, and ensuring on-call teams receive meaningful alerts for immediate response.

9.6 Hands-On Project: Building a Scalable, Resilient Go Microservice

This hands-on project will bring together the chapter's scaling and optimization techniques, focusing on deploying a resilient, high-performing Go microservice.

- **Project Overview and Setup**: Define a microservice with an API endpoint that handles high volumes of requests. This project should include setting up resilience patterns, caching, and performance monitoring.
- **Implementing Load Balancing and Autoscaling**
- Deploy the Go microservice on a Kubernetes cluster with a load balancer configured for round-robin traffic distribution.
- Set up Horizontal Pod Autoscaling (HPA) to automatically scale the service based on CPU or custom metrics, showing how it dynamically adjusts instances to meet demand.
- **Adding Caching and Rate Limiting**
- Implement Redis as a caching layer to store frequently requested data, reducing the load on the primary database.
- Set up rate limiting in the API layer to protect against abuse and optimize the server load, demonstrating rate limit configuration for different types of users.
- **Resilience with Circuit Breakers and Retries**
- Add a circuit breaker pattern to handle dependency failures gracefully, setting thresholds and recovery conditions.
- Configure retry logic with exponential backoff to manage transient failures, providing an example of handling temporary network or service disruptions.
- **Monitoring and Performance Tuning**
- Integrate Prometheus for metrics collection and Grafana for real-time monitoring dashboards, covering CPU, memory, latency, and cache hit rates.
- Enable pprof profiling in the Go microservice and analyze the profiling data to identify performance bottlenecks, optimizing the application based on insights from profiling.
- Set up alerts for key performance metrics, ensuring that any significant drop in performance is flagged immediately.

Advanced Topics and Emerging Trends

10.1 Serverless Architectures with Go

Start by introducing serverless computing as a trend that abstracts infrastructure management, allowing developers to focus purely on code.

- **What is Serverless Architecture?**
- Define serverless architecture as a model where cloud providers manage infrastructure, enabling automatic scaling and billing based on actual usage.
- Discuss how serverless platforms work, detailing benefits like reduced operational overhead, automatic scaling, and cost efficiency.
- **Deploying Go Functions in a Serverless Environment**
- Walk through deploying a Go function to a serverless platform like **AWS Lambda** or **Google Cloud Functions**. Cover the basic setup, showing how Go functions handle incoming requests in a serverless context.
- Provide practical tips on structuring Go code for serverless functions, such as minimizing cold start times, optimizing initialization, and reducing dependencies.
- Discuss the limitations of serverless in cloud-native applications, such as latency during cold starts and the stateless nature of functions, and offer strategies to mitigate these issues.
- **Best Practices for Go Serverless Functions**
- Cover best practices, including error handling, retry policies, and optimizing function sizes.
- Discuss the importance of using external storage and databases for

persisting data, as serverless functions are inherently stateless.

- Provide guidance on monitoring serverless functions, covering tools like AWS CloudWatch for tracing and alerting on performance issues.

10.2 Event-Driven Systems in Cloud-Native Go Applications

Explore event-driven architectures and their increasing relevance in microservices and cloud-native ecosystems.

- **Introduction to Event-Driven Architecture (EDA)**
- Define event-driven architecture, where components communicate by emitting and responding to events. Describe how EDA enables decoupled, scalable, and real-time applications.
- Discuss how EDA is ideal for use cases like real-time analytics, IoT applications, and asynchronous processing in cloud-native environments.
- **Using Message Brokers with Go (e.g., Kafka, NATS)**
- Introduce **Kafka** and **NATS** as popular message brokers for managing event streams and handling high-throughput data processing.
- Walk through setting up a Go application to publish and consume events from Kafka. Cover essential concepts such as topics, partitions, and offsets for Kafka, and subjects for NATS.
- Provide examples of configuring a Go microservice to process events, including error handling and retry strategies.
- **Implementing Event-Driven Microservices with Event Sourcing and CQRS**
- Explain **Event Sourcing**, where state changes are stored as events, enabling a complete history of modifications.
- Introduce the **Command Query Responsibility Segregation (CQRS)** pattern, which separates read and write operations to optimize performance and scalability.
- Provide an example of implementing event sourcing in a Go application, showing how to capture, store, and process events in an event log. Discuss how CQRS can help optimize query performance in data-intensive applications.

10.3 Service Mesh for Secure and Observable Microservices

Introduce the concept of a service mesh, a dedicated infrastructure layer for managing communication between microservices.

- **What is a Service Mesh?**
- Define a service mesh as a framework that provides secure, observable, and reliable communication between microservices.
- Explain how service meshes work by handling traffic routing, load balancing, and monitoring without adding complexity to individual services.
- **Using Istio or Linkerd with Go Microservices**
- Introduce **Istio** and **Linkerd** as popular service mesh options, describing their roles in managing traffic, enforcing policies, and providing observability in microservices.
- Walk through integrating a Go application with Istio, covering service-to-service encryption (mTLS) and traffic control.
- Provide examples of configuring rate limiting, retries, and circuit breaking policies with Istio, demonstrating how service meshes simplify resilience and security for microservices.
- **Enhancing Observability with Service Mesh Telemetry**
- Describe how service meshes offer built-in observability, including request tracing, metrics, and logging.
- Walk through setting up observability with Istio's telemetry tools, such as Prometheus and Grafana for metrics, and Jaeger for tracing.
- Discuss best practices for managing performance overhead, including adjusting sampling rates for tracing and focusing on critical metrics.

10.4 API Security Advancements: OAuth 2.1, OpenID Connect, and Beyond

Discuss the latest developments in API security, focusing on authentication and authorization protocols that enhance security in cloud-native applications.

- **Overview of OAuth 2.1 and OpenID Connect**
- Introduce **OAuth 2.1** as the latest version of the OAuth protocol, which includes stricter security requirements for handling authorization in web and mobile applications.
- Explain **OpenID Connect** (OIDC) as an identity layer on top of OAuth, enabling secure user authentication and single sign-on (SSO) for cloud-native applications.
- **Implementing OAuth 2.1 with Go**
- Walk through setting up OAuth 2.1 in a Go application, demonstrating how to integrate with an identity provider (e.g., Auth0, Okta) for secure authorization.
- Provide examples of configuring authorization grants (e.g., authorization code flow) in a Go API, covering best practices for managing access tokens and refresh tokens securely.
- Discuss how to configure token introspection and revocation, ensuring secure token management in distributed environments.
- **Best Practices for API Security in Cloud-Native Applications**
- Cover API security best practices, such as rate limiting, input validation, and implementing strict authorization policies.
- Provide guidance on using JSON Web Tokens (JWT) for stateless authentication, covering how to issue, validate, and manage JWTs securely.
- Discuss the importance of regularly auditing and updating API security policies, especially as new security vulnerabilities are discovered.

10.5 Emerging Tools and Techniques in Go Development

Highlight emerging tools, techniques, and practices that are becoming popular in the Go development community, especially for cloud-native development.

- **Go Generics and Code Reusability**
- Introduce **Generics** in Go, which became available in Go 1.18, and discuss how they enable type-safe, reusable code.

- Provide examples of using generics in Go functions and data structures, showing how they simplify code and improve maintainability in cloud-native applications.
- Cover best practices for adopting generics in Go, emphasizing scenarios where generics enhance readability and efficiency without adding complexity.
- **Using GraphQL with Go for Flexible APIs**
- Introduce **GraphQL** as an alternative to REST, offering more flexibility in retrieving data by allowing clients to specify exactly what they need.
- Walk through setting up a GraphQL API in Go, using libraries like gqlgen to define schemas, queries, and resolvers.
- Discuss the benefits of GraphQL for microservices and cloud-native applications, especially in scenarios with complex data relationships or multiple clients (e.g., mobile and web applications).
- **The Rise of WebAssembly (Wasm) in Go Applications**
- Explain **WebAssembly (Wasm)** as a binary instruction format that allows Go applications to run at near-native speed in web browsers or server environments.
- Discuss emerging use cases for WebAssembly in Go, such as embedding Wasm modules in cloud applications, enabling cross-platform support, and running secure, sandboxed code.
- Provide an example of compiling Go code to WebAssembly and running it in a browser environment, showcasing its potential in cloud-native applications.

10.6 Hands-On Project: Building a Serverless, Event-Driven Go Application

To consolidate these advanced topics, this hands-on project guides readers in building a serverless, event-driven Go application with modern API security and observability.

- **Project Overview and Architecture**: Define an event-driven application where user actions (e.g., uploads, form submissions) trigger events that are processed in a serverless environment. The application should include an API secured with OAuth 2.1.

- **Setting Up Serverless Functions with AWS Lambda**
- Walk through deploying Go functions on AWS Lambda, setting up an event-based trigger (e.g., S3 upload).
- Demonstrate function optimizations, such as reducing cold start times and structuring the code for efficient execution.
- **Integrating Kafka for Event Streaming**
- Set up a Kafka cluster to handle events generated by user actions and process them asynchronously with Go consumers.
- Implement a Go consumer to process Kafka events, covering strategies for ensuring message durability, ordering, and error handling.
- **Implementing API Security with OAuth 2.1**
- Configure OAuth 2.1 for the API, securing endpoints with access tokens. Integrate a third-party identity provider (e.g., Auth0) for token management.
- Demonstrate API rate limiting and input validation to enhance security.
- **Adding Observability with OpenTelemetry**
- Integrate OpenTelemetry for distributed tracing and Prometheus for monitoring, tracking the end-to-end flow of requests through serverless functions and event streams.
- Set up Grafana dashboards and alerting for key metrics, providing insights into latency, error rates, and system load.

Case Studies and Real-World Applications

11.1 Case Study 1: Building a Scalable E-Commerce Platform with Go
Explore how a large-scale e-commerce platform leveraged Go to build a reliable and highly scalable application.

- **Overview and Requirements**
- Describe the core requirements for an e-commerce platform: high availability, low latency, and efficient handling of high traffic during peak times (e.g., Black Friday sales).
- Highlight key functionalities such as user authentication, product catalog management, shopping cart, payment processing, and order management.
- **Design and Architecture**
- Explain the system architecture, focusing on how the platform was built using a microservices architecture in Go.
- Discuss the choice of Go for services that required low latency and high concurrency, such as handling user sessions, product searches, and order management.
- Describe the infrastructure setup using Kubernetes for container orchestration, with each microservice deployed in isolated containers to scale independently.
- **Challenges and Solutions**
- **Handling High Traffic**: Explain the load-balancing strategy and autoscaling configuration to manage traffic spikes. Discuss the use of Kubernetes' Horizontal Pod Autoscaler to dynamically scale services.

- **Data Consistency and Integrity**: Discuss techniques to manage consistency across services, such as eventual consistency and distributed transactions.
- **Performance Optimization**: Describe how profiling tools like pprof were used to detect bottlenecks in request handling and optimize performance.
- **Results and Key Takeaways**
- Highlight the outcomes, such as increased stability, improved customer experience, and the ability to handle large surges in traffic.
- Summarize lessons learned, emphasizing the importance of efficient concurrency management, load balancing, and proactive scaling.

11.2 Case Study 2: Real-Time Analytics for IoT Data Processing with Go and Kafka

This case study explores a real-time analytics platform built in Go, processing large volumes of IoT data using Kafka.

- **Overview and Requirements**
- Describe the requirements for processing IoT data in real time, including low latency, fault tolerance, and the ability to handle millions of events per second.
- Discuss typical use cases, such as monitoring sensors in smart homes, tracking GPS data for vehicles, or analyzing data from industrial equipment.
- **Design and Architecture**
- Explain the event-driven architecture, detailing the role of Kafka as the messaging backbone that allows services to communicate asynchronously.
- Highlight Go's role in developing lightweight, high-throughput microservices to handle message ingestion, processing, and storage.
- Describe the setup for data storage using time-series databases like InfluxDB or Prometheus, which are optimized for storing and querying large volumes of IoT data.

- **Challenges and Solutions**
- **High Throughput Requirements**: Explain how Go's concurrency model and Kafka's partitioning capabilities were used to manage high event throughput.
- **Fault Tolerance**: Discuss implementing fault tolerance with retry logic, circuit breakers, and data replication across multiple Kafka brokers.
- **Data Processing**: Describe strategies for efficiently processing and transforming data, such as batching, filtering, and aggregating data points.
- **Results and Key Takeaways**
- Summarize the outcomes, including real-time insights generated from IoT data and the ability to scale as the number of connected devices grows.
- Provide key lessons learned, emphasizing Go's suitability for high-performance, concurrent applications in event-driven architectures.

11.3 Case Study 3: Cloud-Native API Gateway for Microservices with Go

Focus on a case study where Go was used to develop an API gateway for a microservices architecture, managing external requests and routing them to the appropriate services.

- **Overview and Requirements**
- Describe the purpose of an API gateway in a microservices architecture: to serve as the single entry point for client requests, perform request validation, and route requests to the correct services.
- Highlight requirements such as security, high availability, request routing, rate limiting, and observability.
- **Design and Architecture**
- Explain the architecture of the API gateway, with Go as the choice language due to its performance and low overhead.
- Discuss the implementation of common gateway features, including authentication (JWT validation), caching, rate limiting, and request logging.

54

- Describe the infrastructure setup in Kubernetes, including integration with service discovery to route requests to available instances of microservices.
- **Challenges and Solutions**
- **Security and Authentication**: Discuss how OAuth 2.1 and JWTs were implemented for secure access control, with middleware to validate tokens.
- **Scaling and Load Management**: Explain load-balancing techniques at the gateway level and how Kubernetes' autoscaling and load balancing were configured.
- **Monitoring and Observability**: Describe how metrics were collected for monitoring request rates, latency, and error rates, using Prometheus and Grafana for visualization.
- **Results and Key Takeaways**
- Highlight the outcomes, including simplified client interactions, enhanced security, and improved scalability.
- Summarize lessons learned, emphasizing the importance of security, monitoring, and efficient request handling in cloud-native API gateways.

11.4 Lessons Learned: Best Practices and Common Pitfalls in Modern App Development

Conclude the chapter with a section summarizing best practices and common pitfalls observed across the case studies. This section will reinforce key takeaways and provide practical guidance for developers.

- **Best Practices**
- **Embrace Concurrency Carefully**: Explain how to manage concurrency for performance gains without overloading system resources. Highlight effective use of goroutines, channels, and worker pools.
- **Prioritize Observability and Monitoring**: Stress the importance of observability from the start, ensuring that metrics, logs, and traces are implemented in every service to enable proactive troubleshooting.
- **Optimize for Scalability and Fault Tolerance**: Describe techniques

for designing scalable services, including load balancing, autoscaling, and the use of service meshes for resilience.

- **Design for Security from Day One**: Reinforce the importance of implementing security at every layer, from authentication and authorization to secure inter-service communication.
- **Common Pitfalls**
- **Underestimating the Complexity of Microservices**: Discuss the tendency to break monoliths into microservices too early, which can lead to increased operational complexity.
- **Ignoring Resource Limits in Kubernetes**: Explain the risks of omitting CPU and memory limits, leading to resource contention and potential service outages.
- **Overusing Dependencies**: Warn against introducing too many external dependencies, which can complicate the stack and increase the risk of dependency failures.
- **Neglecting Error Handling and Retries**: Stress the importance of thorough error handling, retries with exponential backoff, and circuit breaking for fault tolerance.

Troubleshooting and Best Practices

12.1 Common Pitfalls in Cloud-Native Go Development

Identify common issues Go developers face in cloud-native environments and explain how to avoid them.

- **Resource Leaks (Memory and Goroutines)**
- Explain how goroutine and memory leaks occur in Go applications, often due to unclosed resources or improperly managed goroutines.
- Provide tips for detecting these leaks, such as monitoring goroutine counts and profiling memory usage.
- Show how to handle resource cleanup using defer statements and proper cancellation of goroutines with context.
- **Data Races and Concurrency Issues**
- Describe data races and concurrency issues, common in high-performance Go applications.
- Introduce Go's built-in race detector as a tool to detect data races during testing.
- Explain best practices for avoiding race conditions, including using channels for communication and synchronization tools like sync.Mutex when accessing shared resources.
- **Improper Error Handling and Panic Management**
- Discuss how unhandled errors and panics can disrupt application stability.
- Show best practices for error handling in Go, such as wrapping errors for context, returning errors up the call stack, and using structured error

types.
- Explain the importance of using recover to handle panics gracefully and ensure the application continues running or fails safely.

12.2 Debugging Tips and Tools for Go Applications

Provide practical debugging techniques and introduce essential tools for identifying and resolving issues in Go applications.

- **Using Logs Effectively for Debugging**
- Discuss the importance of logging and how to use it to trace issues in cloud-native applications.
- Introduce structured logging with libraries like Logrus or Zap to add context to log entries and make them more searchable.
- Show how to use different log levels (DEBUG, INFO, WARN, ERROR) to filter relevant logs, especially when diagnosing issues in production environments.
- **Profiling with pprof for Performance Analysis**
- Explain how pprof, Go's built-in profiling tool, can help identify CPU, memory, and goroutine bottlenecks.
- Walk through setting up pprof to capture and analyze profiles, covering the use of CPU and memory profiles to spot inefficient code.
- Provide examples of common performance issues identified through pprof, such as high memory usage, inefficient loops, or excessive goroutine creation, and how to address them.
- **Using Delve for Step-by-Step Debugging**
- Introduce **Delve**, Go's debugger, for in-depth analysis and step-by-step code execution.
- Demonstrate how to set breakpoints, inspect variables, and step through code with Delve, especially useful in complex cloud-native applications.
- Discuss using Delve in local and remote debugging sessions, covering configurations to debug applications running in Docker or Kubernetes.

12.3 Solutions to Common Concurrency and Deployment Issues

Provide specific troubleshooting techniques for concurrency-related issues and deployment challenges in cloud-native Go applications.

- **Diagnosing Deadlocks and Goroutine Contention**
- Explain how deadlocks occur in Go, often when multiple goroutines wait indefinitely for each other to release resources.
- Show how to use pprof and race detector to identify deadlocks, and discuss strategies like timeout contexts and channel select statements to prevent them.
- Provide examples of goroutine contention issues and demonstrate how to resolve them by reducing shared resource access or redesigning concurrency patterns.
- **Handling Latency and Network Issues in Distributed Applications**
- Describe latency as a common issue in cloud-native applications, often due to network delays or slow inter-service communication.
- Introduce techniques to diagnose latency, such as distributed tracing with **OpenTelemetry**, which allows visibility into request flow across services.
- Cover strategies to reduce latency, including optimizing gRPC and HTTP/2 settings, implementing caching, and reducing dependency on remote services for critical paths.
- **Deployment Issues and Rollbacks**
- Discuss common deployment issues in Kubernetes, such as configuration errors, failed health checks, and resource limits.
- Provide guidance on troubleshooting failed deployments using Kubernetes commands (kubectl logs, kubectl describe), ensuring a systematic approach to identifying and resolving deployment issues.
- Cover rollback strategies with Kubernetes and Helm, explaining how to quickly revert to a previous version if new deployments cause issues.

12.4 Performance Tuning for Production-Ready Go Applications

Offer best practices for tuning Go applications to ensure high performance and reliability in production.

- **Optimizing Go's Garbage Collector**
- Explain how Go's garbage collector works and its impact on application performance.
- Show how to adjust the garbage collector's behavior with the GOGC environment variable, balancing memory usage and GC frequency.
- Discuss tips for reducing garbage collection overhead, such as reusing objects and avoiding excessive memory allocations in high-throughput applications.
- **Efficient Use of Goroutines and Channels**
- Discuss best practices for goroutines and channels, emphasizing the importance of managing goroutine lifecycles and avoiding excessive concurrency.
- Provide examples of when to use worker pools to control goroutine count, improving CPU and memory efficiency.
- Cover advanced concurrency patterns in Go, such as fan-in and fan-out, to manage task distribution effectively.
- **Reducing Response Latency with Network Optimizations**
- Explain how to optimize networking for Go applications, such as enabling HTTP/2 for reduced latency and using connection pooling.
- Provide examples of tuning HTTP clients for better performance, such as adjusting timeout values, configuring retries, and using persistent connections.
- Discuss when to use gRPC over HTTP for high-performance inter-service communication and how to configure gRPC settings to reduce latency.

12.5 Best Practices for Observability and Incident Management

Discuss essential practices for observability and incident response in cloud-native Go applications, helping teams detect, diagnose, and resolve issues efficiently.

- **Implementing End-to-End Observability**
- Emphasize the importance of observability from development to pro-

duction, using metrics, logs, and traces.

- Guide readers in setting up a structured observability stack with **Prometheus** for metrics, **Grafana** for visualization, and **OpenTelemetry** for tracing.
- Cover best practices for metrics design, such as defining SLOs (Service Level Objectives) and SLIs (Service Level Indicators), to measure application health accurately.

- **Creating Effective Alerts**
- Discuss alerting best practices, including configuring alerts for critical metrics like error rates, latency, and resource usage.
- Explain how to set actionable alert thresholds and reduce alert fatigue by avoiding excessive notifications for low-priority issues.
- Provide tips on structuring alert messages to include context and resolution steps, ensuring faster and more efficient incident responses.

- **Establishing Runbooks and Incident Response Plans**
- Describe runbooks as step-by-step guides for handling incidents, covering common issues like failed deployments, high error rates, and increased latency.
- Discuss the importance of creating incident response plans, with specific roles and procedures for diagnosing and resolving issues.
- Provide a template for a sample runbook, outlining steps for common troubleshooting scenarios, ensuring teams have a systematic approach to incident management.

12.6 Building a Resilient Culture: Continuous Improvement and Learning

Conclude the chapter with a focus on building a resilient culture of continuous improvement and learning, essential for long-term success in cloud-native development.

- **Encouraging Postmortems and Retrospectives**
- Introduce postmortems as a tool for reviewing incidents and identifying root causes, with the goal of continuous learning.

- Discuss how to conduct effective postmortems, focusing on blameless discussions, actionable takeaways, and clear documentation.
- Provide tips on setting up retrospectives after major project milestones, allowing teams to reflect on successes, challenges, and opportunities for improvement.
- **Establishing a Knowledge Base for Common Issues**
- Discuss the value of creating a centralized knowledge base to document solutions for recurring issues, making it easier to onboard new team members and streamline troubleshooting.
- Suggest tools for managing knowledge bases, such as Confluence or GitHub Wiki, and provide examples of essential documentation topics.
- Encourage teams to regularly update documentation, especially as infrastructure or application components evolve.
- **Promoting Collaboration and Cross-Training**
- Highlight the importance of cross-functional knowledge within teams, ensuring developers understand cloud infrastructure and DevOps engineers understand application behavior.
- Suggest cross-training sessions, pair programming, and knowledge-sharing initiatives to build team resilience and improve incident response.
- Discuss the benefits of collaboration in complex cloud-native environments, where effective communication and shared expertise are critical for fast problem resolution.